At the Park

By Sally Cowan

Dad drives me in the car
to the big park.

It's not far from home.

Dad hands me the ball.

Archie and Kate are waiting
for me at the park.

I train and play games
with them.

My coach, Marg,
is at the park, too.

She has a big smile!

Marg gets us to start
with a jog.

I swing my arms and dash
to the goal and back.

Marg brings yellow cones
to the park.

She sets up a cone.

Then we take part
in some drills.

We kick and run to the cone.

Then we go back again.

It can be hard!

Marg sets up more cones.

They are not far from
each other.

Marg tells us to march up to the cones.

We kick to each other.

I kick to Marg.

Next, we try kicking goals.

Kate kicks at the black net.

She swings her arms
and kicks up high.

It's a goal!

But it can be hard to kick goals.

Marg lets me try again.

This time, I kick a goal.

"What a star!" yells Archie.

Then, Dad comes to take me home in the car.

I have great fun at the park!

CHECKING FOR MEANING

1. Who are the boy's friends? *(Literal)*

2. What are two things that Marg gets the boy and his friends to do? *(Literal)*

3. Why does the boy say that it can be hard to kick goals? *(Inferential)*

EXTENDING VOCABULARY

waiting	What is the base of the word *waiting*? How has adding *–ing* changed the meaning of the base?
drills	What is meant by *drills* in the book? When else might you do drills? What else can *drills* mean?
march	What does *march* mean? What other words are used to describe movement in the book? E.g. jog, dash, run.

MOVING BEYOND THE TEXT

1. Why is it important to practise a sport such as soccer?

2. What else can you practise?

3. What is your favourite thing to do at the park? Why?

4. What sort of person does a coach need to be? Why?

SPEED SOUNDS

ar	er	ir	ur	or

PRACTICE WORDS

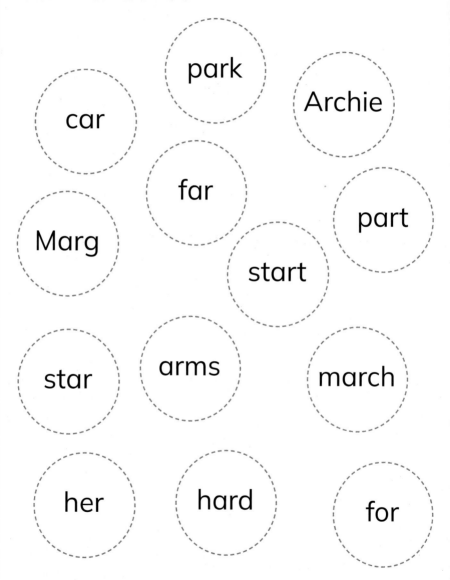

park

car

Archie

far

Marg

part

start

star

arms

march

her

hard

for